FAVORITE BASKETBALL TEAMS

Chicago Bulls

BY ELLEN LABRECQUE

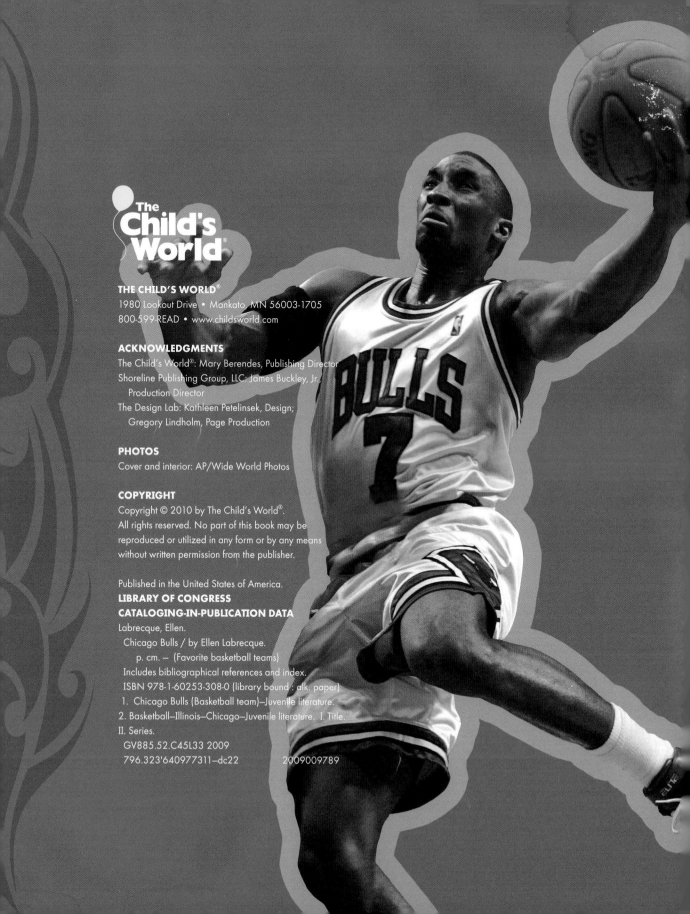

The Child's World

THE CHILD'S WORLD®
1980 Lookout Drive • Mankato, MN 56003-1705
800-599-READ • www.childsworld.com

ACKNOWLEDGMENTS

The Child's World®: Mary Berendes, Publishing Director
Shoreline Publishing Group, LLC: James Buckley, Jr.,
   Production Director
The Design Lab: Kathleen Petelinsek, Design;
   Gregory Lindholm, Page Production

PHOTOS

Cover and interior: AP/Wide World Photos

Published in the United States of America.

LIBRARY OF CONGRESS
CATALOGING-IN-PUBLICATION DATA

Labrecque, Ellen.
  Chicago Bulls / by Ellen Labrecque.
     p. cm. — (Favorite basketball teams)
  Includes bibliographical references and index.
  ISBN 978-1-60253-308-0 (library bound : alk. paper)
  1. Chicago Bulls (Basketball team)—Juvenile literature.
  2. Basketball—Illinois—Chicago—Juvenile literature. I. Title.
II. Series.
  GV885.52.C45L33 2009
  796.323'640977311—dc22   2009009789

Table of Contents

Go, Bulls!

Holy cow! Or should we say *Holy Bulls!* The Chicago Bulls are an awesome basketball team. The greatest basketball player of all time played for the Bulls. This team has fans all over the Midwest. Are you one of those fans? Let's meet the Chicago Bulls!

Slam dunk! Chicago's Tyrus Thomas scores . . . hard!

Great block! Chicago takes on stars like Cleveland's LeBron James.

Who Are the Bulls?

The Chicago Bulls play in the National Basketball Association (NBA). They are one of 30 teams in the NBA. The NBA includes the Eastern Conference and the Western Conference. The Bulls play in the Central Division of the Eastern Conference. The Eastern Conference Champion plays the Western Conference Champion in the **NBA Finals**. The Bulls have won the NBA title six times!

Where They Came From

The Bulls joined the NBA in 1966. They weren't the first pro basketball team to play in Chicago. The Chicago Bruins played in the ABA (American Basketball Association) from 1925 to1931. Two other Chicago teams played in the NBA. They were the Chicago Stags (1949–1950) and the Chicago Packers (1961–1962). Chicago finally got an NBA team to stick around when the Bulls came to town!

9

Almost, but not quite! The Bulls lost to the Lakers in the 1971 playoffs.

10

Games between the Bulls and the Pistons are always tough battles.

Who They Play

The Bulls play 82 games from October to April. They play every other NBA team at least once. The Detroit Pistons are one of the Bulls' biggest **rivals**. The two teams play in the same division. Both have a history of playing tough **defense**. They have met in the playoffs six times. The last time was in the 2007 Eastern Conference **Semifinals**. The Pistons won the series, 4–2.

Where They Play

The Bulls used to play their games in Chicago Stadium. In 1994, they moved across the street to the United Center. This large indoor arena holds 21,711 people. A bronze statue stands in the lobby of the United Center. The statue is of Michael Jordan. Jordan led the Bulls to six NBA titles. Three of the titles were won in Chicago Stadium. The other three were won in the United Center.

Championship banners hang above the Bulls' home court.

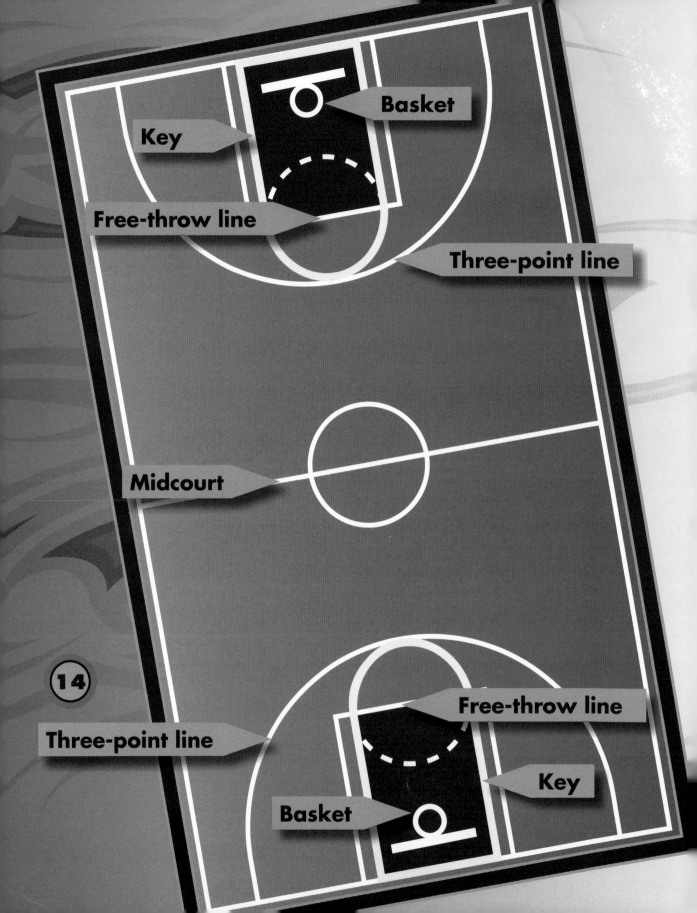

Basket

Key

Free-throw line

Three-point line

Midcourt

Free-throw line

Three-point line

Key

Basket

14

The Basketball Court

Basketball is played on a court made of wood. An NBA court is 94 feet (29 m) long. A painted line shows the middle of the court. Other lines lay out the free-throw area. The space below each basket is known as the "key." The baskets at each end are 10 feet (3 m) off the ground. The metal rims of the baskets stick out over the court. Nylon nets hang from the rims.

Big Days!

The Chicago Bulls have had many great moments, especially in the 1990s. Here are three of the greatest:

1991: The Bulls won their first NBA championship.

1993: Chicago became the first NBA team in 27 seasons to win three championships in a row. Michael Jordan was named Finals Most Valuable Player for the third straight season.

1998: The Bulls won their third straight title . . . again! Jordan led the NBA in scoring for the tenth time!

Star Michael Jordan (left) and coach Phil Jackson led the Bulls to six titles.

The Bulls found themselves down in more ways than one in 2001.

Tough Days!

The Bulls can't win all their games. Some games or seasons don't turn out well. The players keep trying to play their best, though! Here are some of the toughest seasons in Bulls history:

1984: The Bulls won only 27 games and lost 55. It was the second worst record in team history.

2001: Chicago won only 15 games. There was a good reason—they had the youngest players in NBA history. Most of them were only 22 years old.

2004: The Bulls missed the playoffs for the sixth straight season. Bulls fans didn't lose hope! The team made the playoffs in 2005.

Meet the Fans

Did you know that President Barack Obama is a Bulls fan? He lived and worked in Chicago for many years. President Obama will be the first to tell you: Chicago is one cold city during the winter! That is why indoor basketball is the perfect sport for this city. Bulls fans can stay warm while cheering for their team.

21

Can you see the Bulls' most famous fan in the background?

22

Jordan was famous for his high-flying slam dunks.

Heroes Then...

The best NBA player ever was Michael Jordan. Jordan could do it all. He could score lots of points and play defense. He could also leap high into the air for slam dunks. **Guard** Scottie Pippen was Jordan's sidekick. He was also a star in his own right. Jerry Sloan played for the Bulls in the 1960s and 1970s. Sloan played great defense. Later, he became one of the NBA's best coaches. Star **forward** Bob Love also played around this time. Love could shoot very well with either hand.

Heroes Now....

Ben Gordon joined the Bulls in 2004. He helped the **offense** with his long-range scoring. In 2008, he became a starter. Derrick Rose was the first pick in the 2008 **NBA Draft**. He fools defenders with slow and steady play. Then, *zoom!* He speeds up and zips right past them. He's also one of the best young passers the NBA has ever seen. Together, these two guards hope to bring the Bulls back to their glory days.

Ben Gordon led the Bulls to the playoffs in 2009.

Gearing Up

Chicago Bulls players wear a uniform and special basketball sneakers. Some wear other pads to protect themselves. Check out this picture of Ben Gordon and learn about what NBA players wear.

The Basketball

NBA basketballs are made of leather. Several pieces are held together with rubber edges. Inside the leather ball is a hollow ball of rubber. This is filled with air. The leather is covered with little bumps called "pebbles." The pebbles help players get a good grip on the ball. The basketball used in the Women's National Basketball Association (WNBA) is slightly smaller than the men's basketball.

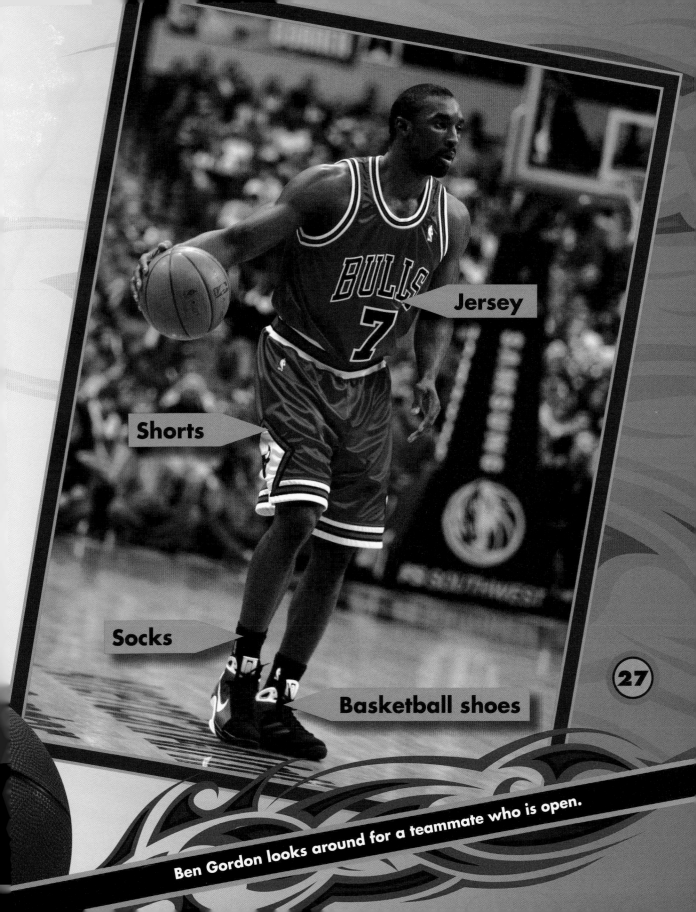

Jersey

Shorts

Socks

Basketball shoes

Ben Gordon looks around for a teammate who is open.

Sports Stats

Note: All numbers shown are through the 2008–2009 season.

HIGH SCORERS

These players have scored the most points for the Bulls.

PLAYER	POINTS
Michael Jordan	29,277
Scottie Pippen	15,123

HELPING HAND

Here are Chicago's all-time leaders in **assists.**

PLAYER	ASSISTS
Michael Jordan	5,012
Scottie Pippen	4,494

CLEANING THE BOARDS

Rebounds are a big part of the game. Here are the Bulls' best rebounders.

PLAYER	REBOUNDS
Michael Jordan	5,836
Tom Boerwinkle	5,745

MOST THREE-POINT SHOTS MADE

Shots taken from behind a line about 23 feet (7 m) from the basket are worth three points. Here are the Bulls' best at these long-distance shots.

PLAYER	THREE-POINT SHOTS
Ben Gordon	770
Kirk Hinrich	708

COACH

Who coached the Bulls to the most wins?

Phil Jackson, 545

Glossary

assists passes to teammates that lead directly to making baskets

defense when a team doesn't have the ball and is trying to keep the other team from scoring

forward one of two tall players who rebound and score near the basket

guard one of two players who set up plays, pass to teammates closer to the basket, and shoot from farther away

NBA Draft a meeting of all the NBA teams at which they choose college players to join them

NBA Finals the seven-game NBA championship series, in which the champion must win four games

offense when a team has the ball and is trying to score

playoffs a series of games between 16 teams that decide which two teams will play in the NBA Finals

rebounds missed shots that bounce off the backboard or rim and are often grabbed by another player

rivals teams that play each other often and have an ongoing competition

semifinals the final round of the playoffs, with the winners going on to play in the final game or series

slam dunk a shot in which a player stuffs the ball into the basket

Find Out More

Books

Christopher, Matt. *Greatest Moments in Basketball History*. New York: Little, Brown, 2009.

Craats, Rennay. *Basketball*. Toronto: Weigl Publishers, 2008.

Hareas, John. *Eyewitness Basketball*. New York: DK, 2005.

Web Sites

Visit our Web page for links about the Chicago Bulls and other NBA teams:

childsworld.com/links

Note to Parents, Teachers, and Librarians: We routinely verify our Web links to make sure they are safe, active sites—so encourage your readers to check them out!

Index

ELLEN LABRECQUE

Ellen Labrecque has written books for young readers on basketball, tennis, ice hockey, and other sports. Ellen used to work for *Sports Illustrated Kids* magazine and has written about many NBA stars. She likes to watch basketball. The Philadelphia 76ers are her favorite team.